MILNER CRAFT SERIES

Knit-a-saurus
Cute & Cuddly Monsters

DONALD ARTHARS

First published in 1994 by
Sally Milner Publishing Pty Ltd
558 Darling Street
Rozelle NSW 2039
Australia

© Donald Arthars 1994

Design and illustrations by Kerrilyn O'Donnell
Photography by Andrew Elton
Styling by Louise Owens
Colour Separated in Australia by Litho Platemakers Pty Ltd
Printed in Australia by Impact Printing Pty Ltd

National Library of Australia
Cataloguing-in-Publication data:

Arthars, Donald.
   Knit-a-saurus.

   ISBN 1 86351 126 1.

   1. Knitting - Patterns. 2. Soft toy making - Patterns. I. Title.
   (Series: Milner craft series).

745.5924

CONTENTS

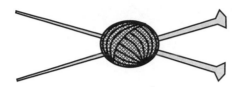

INTRODUCTION

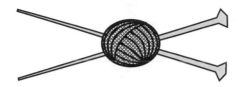

Sixty-five million years ago they roamed the earth and terrified lesser creatures. They're back! But now they will delight any child – they're big, beautiful, and cuddly. The distinctive features of some of the most popular and well known prehistoric creatures have been very simply captured in these designs and any young enthusiast will instantly recognise his or her favourite.

T. Rex is here and stands tall and terrible with white sharp teeth in a great big grin. Stegosaurus has his large spinal plates that shade him from the hot sun. And Triceratops has a large neck frill to thrill and frighten. Pterodactyl, although not a real dinosaur, is certainly a famous prehistoric performer and has a starring role in this cast. They're gathered together in this book to make a big noise at your place soon. They can be knitted in the more lifelike tones of wool or you could let your imagination loose and use some of the wild and bright colours now available. They'll be treasured friends for anyone for ages to come.

I hope you have a great deal of fun applying your artistic flair to the creation of these wonderful creatures.

Enjoy !

Donald

KEY TO SYMBOLS

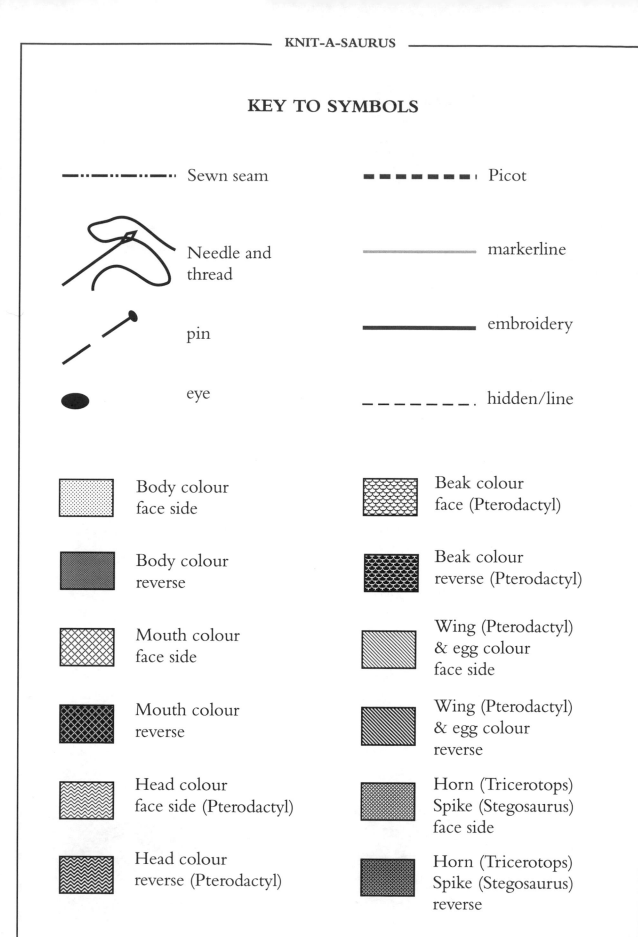

—··—··—··—··—·· Sewn seam

Needle and thread

pin

eye

▪ ▬ ▬ ▬ ▬ ▬ ▬ ▪ Picot

—————————— markerline

—————————— embroidery

— — — — — — — hidden/line

Body colour
face side

Body colour
reverse

Mouth colour
face side

Mouth colour
reverse

Head colour
face side (Pterodactyl)

Head colour
reverse (Pterodactyl)

Beak colour
face (Pterodactyl)

Beak colour
reverse (Pterodactyl)

Wing (Pterodactyl)
& egg colour
face side

Wing (Pterodactyl)
& egg colour
reverse

Horn (Tricerotops)
Spike (Stegosaurus)
face side

Horn (Tricerotops)
Spike (Stegosaurus)
reverse

METHOD

MATERIAL REQUIREMENTS

For each of the models you will need approximately 100 g of 8 ply yarn and 350 g of filling, unless otherwise indicated.

The filling should be clean, non-allergenic material, suitable for young children. Crumbed foam can be used if the fine material is removed, but polyester fibre filling is much easier to work with and gives a much better finish.

You will also need:

- one pair of 3 mm (No 11) knitting needles (30 cm length is fine for most work)

- one pair of 5 mm (No 6) knitting needles is required in some cases (check the specific pattern before starting)

- a sharp, fine knitter's needle or darning needle for sewing

- long dressmaker's pins, with pearl heads so they are easily seen

- a tapered stick (something similar to a 12 mm dowel with a rounded blunt end) for pushing the filling into tight corners

- small scissors for trimming ends, cutting yarn, etc

MEASUREMENT CONVERSIONS

Centimetres (cm) are used. To convert to inches, divide the measurement by 2.5 (2½). Conversely, to convert inches to centimetres, simply multiply the figure by 2.5. For example, 5 cm is approx. 2 inches.

TENSION

Check your tension before commencing. Using 3 mm needles and 8 ply yarn, work a square of st st over 35 sts. Pin the square out flat without stretching – 26 sts across the work should measure 10 cm. If you have more sts to 10 cm, use larger needles. If you have less sts to 10 cm, use smaller needles.

ABBREVIATIONS

The abbreviations used are fairly standard within the knitting world. Alt: alternate; beg: begin/ning; cont: continue, continuing; dec: decrease/s, decreasing; foll: following, follows; inc: increase/s, increasing; K: knit; P: purl; psso: pass slipped stitch over; rem: remain/s, remainder/ remaining; rep: repeat; sl: slip; st/s: stitch/es; st st: stocking stitch (knit all sts on right side of work, purl all sts on wrong side of work); tog: together; yfwd: yarn forward (bring yarn under needle then over into knitting position again, thus forming a stitch).

BRACKETED INSTRUCTIONS

Any instructions within brackets are to be repeated the number of times indicated immediately after the brackets.

Fig 1

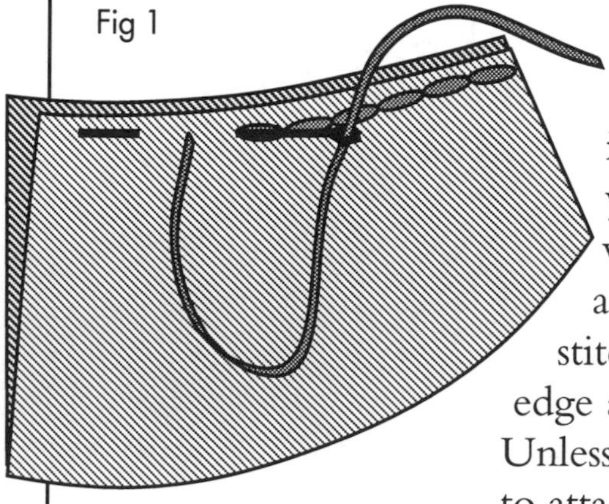

ASSEMBLY INSTRUCTIONS

Unless otherwise indicated, follow these instructions. For the larger pieces, use matching yarn when sewing up. Pieces should be placed with right sides together, matching the shaping and without stretching the work. Use back stitch (see fig 1), working one stitch in from the edge and leaving a gap, where indicated, for turning. Unless otherwise stated, use matching sewing thread to attach smaller pieces.

Legs

In most cases, the Legs were started at the base of the foot (see fig 2a, 2b and 2c). Draw up the cast on sts to form a flat base. For added support, insert a flat disc of plastic, approximately 3.5 cm in diameter, before filling. The discs can be cut from soft drink bottles or milk containers. Make sure there are no rough areas around the edges of the discs.

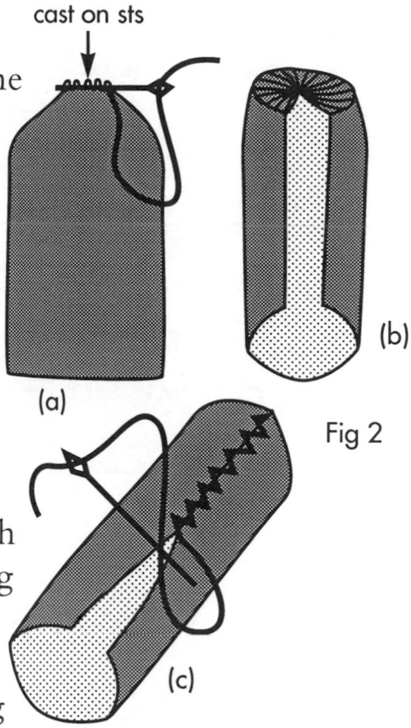

cast on sts

(a)

(b)

(c)

Fig 2

Filling

Try to fill the work evenly, allowing each batch of filling to blend in with the filling already in place (this will stop the finished work from looking lumpy). Fill the model firmly without stretching the knitting unduly (see fig 3), bearing in mind that the filling will settle a little with use. Add a little more filling when closing the gaps left in seams and when attaching limbs.

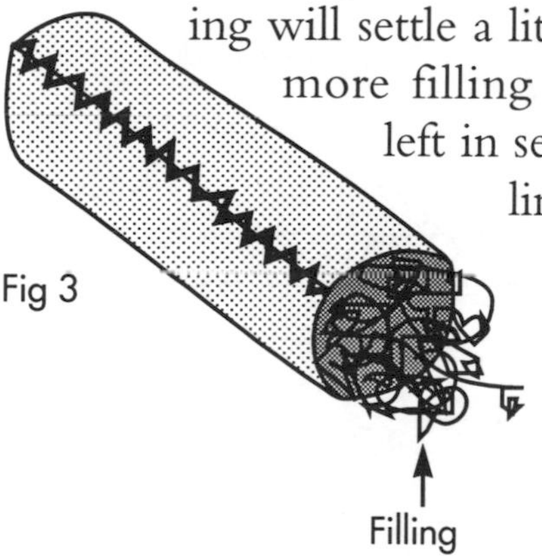

Fig 3

Filling

Positioning Limbs

In most instances, there will be measurements given for the positioning of limbs (see example over the page). Use these in the following manner: measure the indicated distance, or count the relevant number of stitches and rows from the given point and mark with a pin. Indications will be given for the upper and lower edges of the limb opening (similar to attaching a sleeve to a garment). Pin the limb to

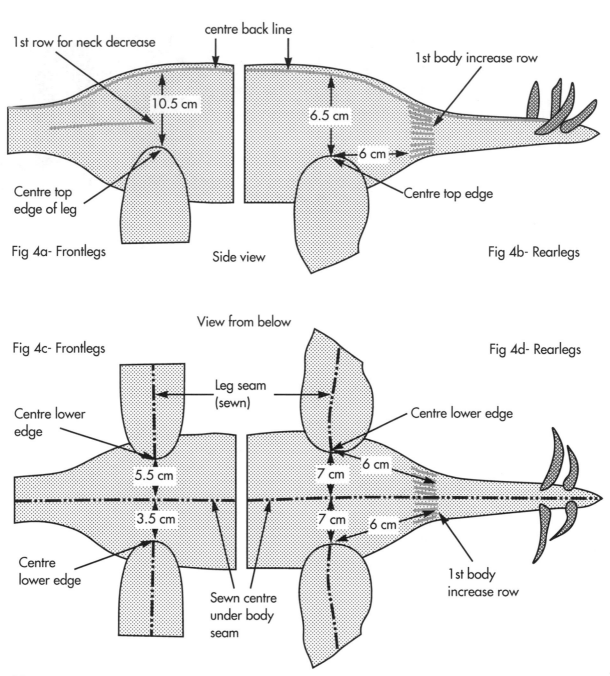

1st row for neck decrease

centre back line

1st body increase row

10.5 cm

6.5 cm

6 cm

Centre top edge of leg

Centre top edge

Fig 4a- Frontlegs

Side view

Fig 4b- Rearlegs

View from below

Fig 4c- Frontlegs

Fig 4d- Rearlegs

Leg seam (sewn)

Centre lower edge

Centre lower edge

5.5 cm

7 cm

6 cm

3.5 cm

7 cm

6 cm

Centre lower edge

1st body increase row

Sewn centre under body seam

Note:
The measurements here are based on those for Stegosaurus, but the method is common to all.

these markings as securely as possible. Stand the model and check for appearance and balance. Adjust as required, a little at a time, until a satisfactory look has been achieved, then stitch in place.

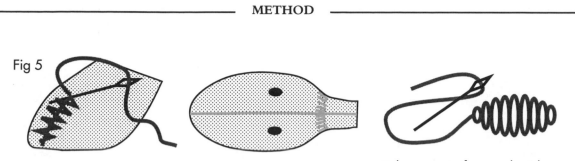

Fig 5

Enlargement of eye embroidery

Embroidery

In a few models, embroidery can be used to enhance the appearance by the addition of claws, and so on (see fig 5). Secure the embroidery thread within the filling before beginning stitches. For claw loops, secure thread and allow a loop to be formed that is approximately 1 cm in length. Secure this and then wind the thread around it a number of times to build the claw. Pass the thread through the loop a few times to secure.

SAFETY

Most of these models have large pieces which should be safe for little children. For younger children, keep in mind that small, loose pieces are unsuitable. Ensure that all attachments are securely joined. For safety's sake, never sew or glue on small embellishments, such as sequins, beads, buttons and so on (see fig 6).

Fig 6

NOTE

The patterns appear in the order of difficulty in making. If you are a knitting novice, start with Brachiosaurus, which is the easiest and then progress to Triceratops, and so on.

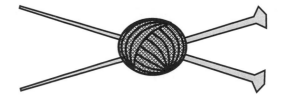

BRACHIOSAURUS

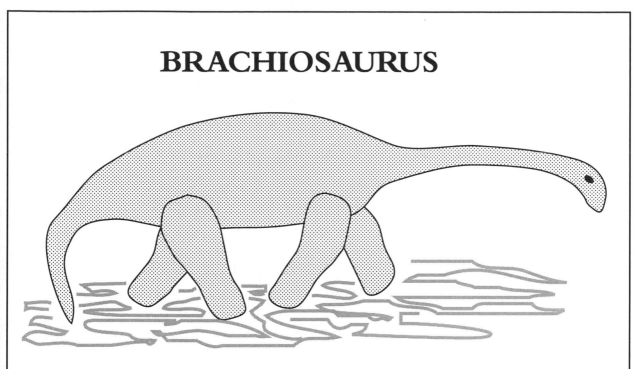

This model stands approximately 42 cm high and 68 cm long.

Materials

Approximately 100 g of 8 ply yarn in selected colour. One pair of 3 mm knitting needles. Filling. Scraps of black yarn for eyes.

TAIL, BODY, NECK AND HEAD

Worked in one piece, beg at tip of tail.

Cast on 4 sts.

1st row (wrong side). Inc knitways in every st...8 sts.

Working in st st, beg with a knit row, inc one st at each end of every 8th row until there are 22 sts, then in every 4th row until there are 30 sts.

Shape body.

Next row. K5, inc in each of next 20 sts, K5...50 sts.

Next row. Purl.

Next row. K20, inc in each of next 10 sts, K20...60 sts.

Work 65 rows st st, beg with a purl row.

Shape for neck.

1st row. K18, K2tog, (K8, K2tog) 3 times, K10...56 sts.

2nd and foll alt rows. Purl.

3rd row. K10, K2tog, K14, K2tog, (K7, K2tog) twice, K10...52 sts.

5th row. K16, K2tog, (K6, K2tog) 3 times, K10...48 sts.

7th row. (K10, K2tog) twice, (K5, K2tog) twice, K10...44 sts.

9th row. K14, K2tog, (K4, K2tog)

3 times, K10...40 sts.

11th row. K10, K2tog, K6, K2tog, (K3, K2tog) twice, K10...36 sts.

13th row. K12, K2tog, (K2, K2tog) 3 times, K10...32 sts.

Work 5 rows st st, beg with a purl row.

19th row. Inc in each of next 3 sts, K5, (K2tog) 8 times, K5, inc in each of next 3 sts...30 sts.

Cont in st st, beg with a purl row, dec one st at beg of next 9 rows...21 sts.

Work 60 rows st st.

Shape head.

1st row. (K2tog) twice, inc in each of next 13 sts, (K2tog) twice...30 sts.

Work 11 rows st st, beg with a purl row.

13th row. (K8, inc in each of next 3 sts) twice, K8...36 sts.

Work 7 rows st st, beg with a purl row.

21st row. K2tog, K9, sl 1, K1, psso, K2tog, K6, sl 1, K1, psso, K2tog, K9, K2tog...30 sts.

Work 5 rows st st, beg with a purl row.

27th row. K2tog, K7, sl 1, K1, psso, K2tog, K4, sl 1, K1, psso, K2tog, K7, K2tog...24 sts.

Work 5 rows st st, beg with a purl row.

33rd row. K2tog, K5, sl 1, K1, psso, K2tog, K2, sl 1, K1, psso, K2tog, K5, K2tog...18 sts.

Work 5 rows st st, beg with a purl row.

39th row. *K2tog, K1; rep from * to end...12 sts.

Work 5 rows st st, beg with a purl row.

45th row. *K2tog, K1; rep from * to end...8 sts.

Break off yarn, thread end through rem sts, draw up and fasten off securely.

To sew up body

Fold in half lengthways with right sides tog. Sew row ends tog, working from tip of nose to centre of body, then from tip of tail to centre of body, leaving a large gap in centre for filling (see fig 1 & 2). Turn to right side and fill firmly, starting at tip of nose and tip of tail and working towards the middle.

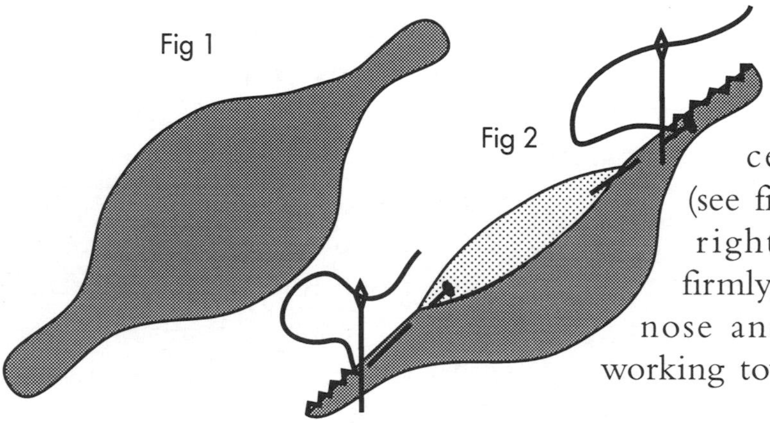

Fig 1

Fig 2

Pin gap closed. The model's circumference should be approximately 38.5 cm at the widest part at this stage (see fig 3). Stitch gap closed.

Fig 3

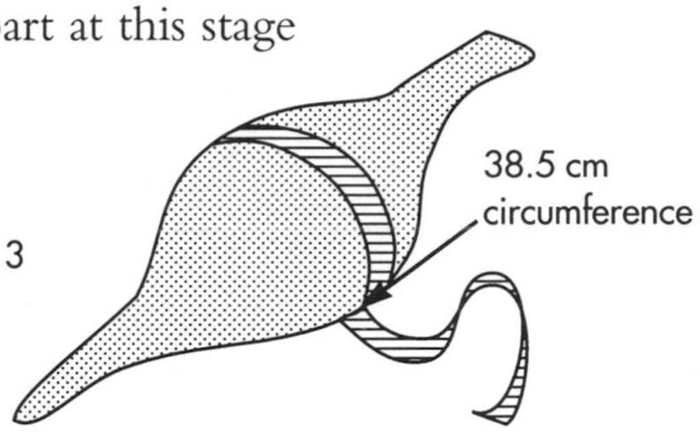

38.5 cm circumference

FRONT LEGS

Make 2, beg at base of foot.
Cast on 10 sts.
1st row (right side). Inc knitways in every st...20 sts.
Work 2 rows st st, beg with a purl row.
Shape toe edge.
Purl 3 rows.★★
Work 48 rows st st, beg with a knit row.
Shape top.
Cont in st st, cast off 3 sts at beg of next 2 rows, then dec one st at each end of foll 4 rows...6 sts.
Next row. (K2tog) 3 times...3 sts. Cast off.

BACK LEFT LEG

Work as for Front Legs to ★★.
Work 18 rows st st, beg with a knit row.
Shape Knee A.
Next row. K3, (K2tog) twice, K6, inc in each of next 4 sts, K3...22 sts.
Work 11 rows st st, beg with a purl row.
Shape Knee B.
Next row. K3, inc in each of next

2 sts, K6, (K2tog) 4 times, K3...20 sts.
Next row. Purl.
Cont in st st, inc one st at each end of next and foll alt rows 6 times in all...32 sts.
Next row. Purl.
Shape top.
Cont in st st, cast off 5 sts at beg of next 2 rows, then dec one st at each end of foll 5 rows...12 sts.
Next row. Purl.
Next row. (K2tog) 6 times...6 sts.
Next row. Purl.
Next row. (K2tog) 3 times...3 sts. Cast off.

BACK RIGHT LEG

Work as for Back Left Leg, noting to work Knee A and Knee B rows as folls.
Shape Knee A.
Next row. K3, inc in each of next 4 sts, K6, (K2tog) twice, K3...22 sts.
Shape Knee B.
Next row. K3, (K2tog) 4 times, K6, inc in each of next 2 sts, K3...20 sts.

To sew up Legs

Slip a length of matching yarn through sts in cast on row, draw up tightly and fasten off to form base of foot. Fold work in half lengthways, with right sides tog, and back stitch over row ends, starting at bottom of Leg and finishing at beg of top shaping. Turn to right side and fill firmly, forming a flat edge from base of foot to toe edge.

TO ASSEMBLE

Pin centre top edge of Front Legs 8.5 cm from centre back and in line with first neck dec row. Pin centre lower edge (leg seam) of Front Legs 4 cm from underbody seam and in line with first neck dec row. Pin centre top edge of Back Legs 5 cm from centre back and 2 cm from first body inc row. Pin centre lower edge (leg seam) 5.5 cm from under-body seam and 5 cm from first body inc row. Check for appearance and stance, adjust if necessary, then stitch in place. Using black yarn, work small sts for eyes just in front of, and either side of, the inc bumps on the head.

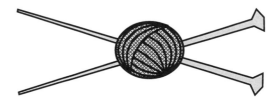

TRICERATOPS

This model stands approximately 17 cm high and 45 cm long.

Materials

Approximately 85 g of 8 ply yarn in selected main colour. One pair of 3 mm knitting needles. Filling. 10 g of white yarn for horns. A remnant of yarn in a contrasting colour for neck frill. Scraps of black yarn for eyes.

Note: Use selected main colour unless otherwise stated.

TAIL, BODY, NECK AND HEAD

Worked in one piece, beg at tip of tail.

Cast on 4 sts.

1st row (wrong side). Inc knitways in every st...8 sts.

Working in st st, beg with a knit row, inc one st at each end of every 4th row until there are 22 sts, then in every 2nd row until there are 30 sts.

Shape for body.

Next row. K5, inc in each of next 20 sts, K5...50 sts.

Next row. Purl.

Next row. K20, inc in each of next 10 sts, K20...60 sts.

Work 65 rows st st, beg with a purl row.

Shape for neck.

1st row. K18, K2tog, (K8, K2tog) 3 times, K10...56 sts.

2nd and foll alt rows. Purl.

3rd row. K10, K2tog, K14, K2tog, (K7, K2tog) twice, K10...52 sts.

5th row. K16, K2tog, (K6, K2tog) 3 times, K10...48 sts.

7th row. (K10, K2tog) twice, (K5, K2tog) twice, K10...44 sts.

9th row. K14, K2tog, (K4, K2tog) 3 times, K10...40 sts.

11th row. K10, K2tog, K6, K2tog, (K3, K2tog) twice, K10...36 sts.

13th row. K12, K2tog, (K2, K2tog) 3 times, K10...32 sts.

14th row. P2tog, purl to last 2 sts, P2tog...30 sts.

Beg with a knit row, work 12 rows st st.

Shape head.

1st row. K11, inc in each of next 3 sts, K2, inc in each of next 3 sts, K11...36 sts.

Work 7 rows st st, beg with a purl row.

9th row. K2tog, K9, sl 1, K1, psso, K2tog, K6, sl 1, K1, psso, K2tog, K9, K2tog...30 sts.

Work 3 rows st st, beg with a purl row.

13th row. K2tog, K7, sl 1, K1, psso, K2tog, K4, sl 1, K1, psso, K2tog, K7, K2tog...24 sts.

Work 3 rows st st, beg with a purl row.

17th row. K2tog, K5, sl 1, K1, psso, K2tog, K2, sl 1, K1, psso, K2tog, K5, K2tog...18 sts.

Work 3 rows st st, beg with a purl row.

21st row. *K2tog, K1; rep from * to end...12 sts.

Work 3 rows st st, beg with a purl row.

25th row. *K2tog, K1; rep from * to end...8 sts.

Break off yarn, thread end through rem sts, draw up and fasten off securely.

To sew up body
Fold in half lengthways with right sides tog. Sew row ends tog, working from tip of nose to centre of body, then from tip of tail to centre body, leaving a large gap in centre for filling. Turn to right side and fill firmly, starting at tip of nose and tip of tail and working towards the middle. Pin gap closed. The model's circumference should be approximately 38.5 cm at the widest part at this stage. Stitch gap closed.

FRONT LEGS

Make 2, beg at base of foot.
Cast on 10 sts.
1st row. Inc knitways in every st...20 sts.
Work 2 rows st st, beg with a purl row.
Shape toe edge.
Purl 3 rows.★★
Work 24 rows st st, beg with a knit row.
Shape top.
Cont in st st, cast off 3 sts at beg of next 2 rows, then dec one st at each end of foll 4 rows...6 sts.
Next row. (K2tog) 3 times...3 sts. Cast off.

BACK LEFT LEG

Work as for Front Legs to ★★.
Work 18 rows st st, beg with a knit row.
Shape Knee A.
Next row. K3, (K2tog) twice, K6, inc in each of next 4 sts, K3...22 sts.
Work 11 rows st st, beg with a purl row.
Shape Knee B.
Next row. K3, inc in each of next 2 sts, K6, (K2tog) 4 times, K3...20 sts.
Next row. Purl.
Cont in st st, inc one st at each end of next and foll alt rows 6 times in all...32 sts.
Next row. Purl.

Shape top.
Cont in st st, cast off 5 sts at beg of next 2 rows, then dec one st at each end of foll 5 rows...12 sts.
Next row. Purl.
Next row. (K2tog) 6 times...6 sts.
Next row. Purl.
Next row. (K2tog) 3 times...3 sts. Cast off.

BACK RIGHT LEG

Work as for Back Left Leg, noting to work Knee A and Knee B rows as folls.
Shape Knee A.
Next row. K3, inc in each of next 4 sts, K6, (K2tog) twice, K3...22 sts.
Shape Knee B.
Next row. K3, (K2tog) 4 times, K6, inc in each of next 2 sts, K3...20 sts.

To sew up Legs
Slip a length of matching yarn through sts in cast on row, draw up tightly and fasten off to form base of foot. Fold work in half lengthways, with right sides tog, and back stitch over rows ends, starting at bottom of Leg and finishing at beg of top shaping. Turn to right side and fill firmly, forming a flat edge from base of foot to toe edge.

HORNS

Make 2 Large Horns as folls.
Using white yarn, cast on 13 sts.
Work 3 rows st st, beg with a purl row.
Cont in st st, dec one st at beg of next and every foll row until 2 sts rem.

Break off yarn, thread end through rem sts, draw up and fasten off securely. See fig 1.

Make 1 Small Horn as folls.

Using white yarn, cast on 12 sts.
Work 3 rows st st, beg with a purl row.
Next row. *K2, K2tog; rep from * to end...9 sts.
Work 3 rows st st, beg with a purl row.
Next row. *K1, K2tog; rep from * to end...6 sts.

Break off yarn, thread end through rem sts, draw up and fasten off securely. See fig 1.

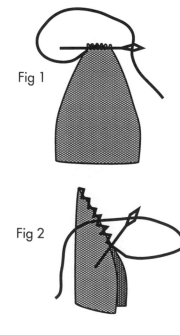

Fig 1

Fig 2

To sew up Horns
With right sides facing out, neatly sew row ends tog from tip to base; fill. See fig 2.

NECK FRILL

Using main colour, cast on 106 sts. Work 4 rows st st, beg with a purl row.

Break off main colour.

Join in 2 strands (to be worked tog) of contrast colour and work picot row as folls.

5th row (picot edge, wrong side). K2tog, *yfwd, K2tog; rep from * to end...105 sts.

Break off contrast colour.

Rejoin one strand of main colour and cont as folls.

6th row. (right side). Knit to last st, inc in last st...106 sts.

7th and foll alt rows. Purl.

8th row. (K2tog, K13) twice, K46, (K13, K2tog) twice...102 sts.

10th row. (K2tog, K12) twice, K2tog, K18, K2tog, K2, sl 1, K1, psso, K18, sl 1, K1, psso, (K12, K2tog) twice...94 sts.

12th row. (K2tog, K11) twice, K42, (K11, K2tog) twice...90 sts.

14th row. (K2tog, K10) twice, K2tog, K16, K2tog, K2, sl 1, K1, psso, K16, sl 1, K1, psso, (K10, K2tog) twice...82 sts.

16th row. (K2tog, K9) twice, K38, (K9, K2tog) twice...78 sts.

18th row. (K2tog, K8) twice, K2tog, K14, K2tog, K2, sl 1, K1, psso, K14, sl 1, K1, psso, (K8, K2tog) twice...70 sts.

20th row. (K2tog, K7) twice, K34, (K7, K2tog) twice...66 sts.

22nd row. (K2tog, K6) twice, K2tog, K12, K2tog, K2, sl 1, K1, psso, K12, sl 1, K1, psso, (K6, K2tog) twice...58 sts.

24th row. (K2tog, K5) twice, K30, (K5, K2tog) twice...54 sts.

26th row. (K2tog, K4) twice, K2tog, K10, K2tog, K2, sl 1, K1, psso, K10, sl 1, K1, psso, (K4, K2tog) twice...46 sts.

28th row. (K2tog, K3) twice, K26, (K3, K2tog) twice...42 sts.

30th row. (K2tog, K2) twice, K2tog, K8, K2tog, K2, sl 1, K1, psso, K8, sl 1, K1, psso, (K2, K2tog) twice...34 sts.

32nd row. (K2tog, K1) twice, K22, (K1, K2tog) twice...30 sts.

34th row. (K2tog) 3 times, K6, K2tog, K2, sl 1, K1, psso, K6, sl 1, K1, psso, (K2tog) twice...22 sts.

35th row. Purl.

Cast off.

Fig 3

←10.5 cm→

←8 cm→

Fig 4

TO ASSEMBLE

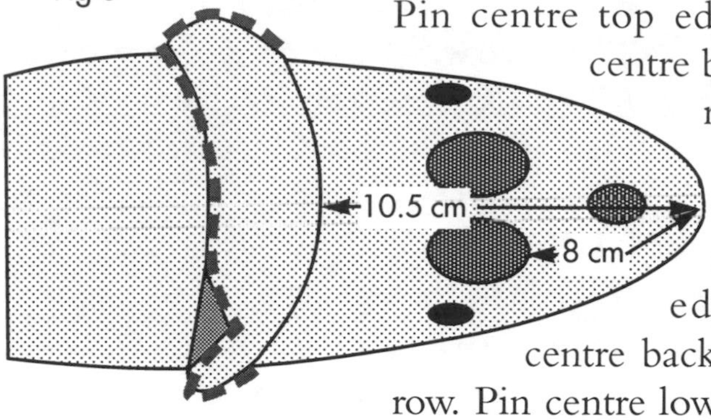

Pin centre top edge of Front Legs 10.5 cm from centre back and in line with first neck dec row. Pin centre lower edge (leg seam) of Front Legs 2 cm from under-body seam and in line with first neck dec row. Pin centre top edge of Back Legs 6.5 cm from centre back and 4 cm in from first body inc row. Pin centre lower edge (leg seam) of Back Legs 5 cm from under-body seam and 7 cm in from first body inc row. Check for appearance and stance, adjust if necessary, then stitch in place.

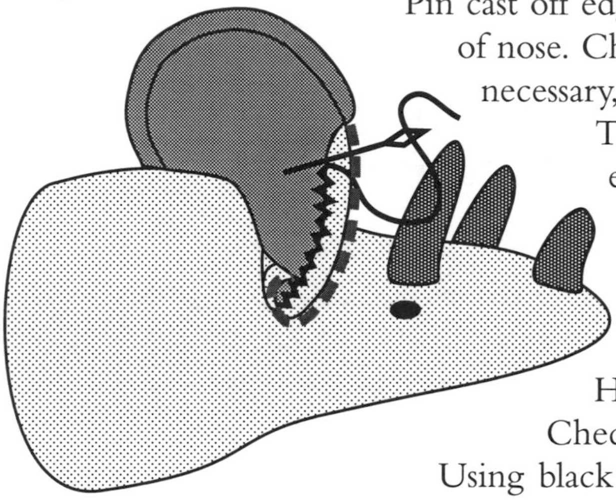

Pin cast off edge of Neck Frill 10.5 cm from tip of nose. Check for look and balance, adjust if necessary, then stitch in place (see fig 3).

Turn Frill to wrong side at picot edge and stitch in place (see fig 4).

Pin the two Large Horns about 8 cm from tip of nose over st decs on top of head, and with 3 clear sts between. Pin the Small Horn on the st dec on the nose. Check appearance and stitch in place .

Using black yarn, work small sts for eyes just below Large Horns on either side of head.

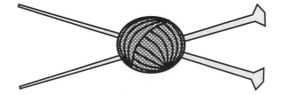

STEGOSAURUS

This model stands approximately 28 cm high and 56 cm long.

Materials

Approximately 100 g of 8 ply yarn for body. One pair of 3 mm knitting needles. Filling. Remnant of white yarn for tail spikes. Scraps of black yarn for eyes.

TAIL, BODY, NECK AND HEAD

Worked in one piece, beg at tip of tail.

Using body yarn, cast on 4 sts.

1st row (wrong side). Inc knit-ways in every st...8 sts.

Work 4 rows st st, beg with a knit row.

6th row. Inc in first st, knit to last st, inc in last st...10 sts.

7th row. Purl.

8th row. (K2, yfwd, K2tog) twice, K2...10 sts.

Work 3 rows st st, beg with a purl row.

12th row. Inc in first st, K1, yfwd, K2tog, K2, yfwd, K2tog, K1, inc in last st...12 sts.

Cont in st st, beg with a purl row, inc one st at each end of every 5th row until there are 22 sts, then at each end of foll 3rd rows until there are 30 sts.

Shape for body.

1st row. K5, inc in each of next

20 sts, K5...50 sts.
2nd row. Purl.
3rd row. K20, inc in each of next 10 sts, K20...60 sts.
Work 65 rows st st, beg with a purl row.
Shape for neck.
1st row. K18, K2tog, (K8, K2tog) 3 times, K10...56 sts.
2nd and foll alt rows. Purl.
3rd row. K10, K2tog, K14, K2tog, (K7, K2tog) twice, K10...52 sts.
5th row. K16, K2tog, (K6, K2tog) 3 times, K10...48 sts.
7th row. (K10, K2tog) twice, (K5, K2tog) twice, K10...44 sts.
9th row. K14, K2tog, (K4, K2tog) 3 times, K10...40 sts.
11th row. K10, K2tog, K6, K2tog, (K3, K2tog) twice, K10...36 sts.
13th row. K12, K2tog, (K2, K2tog) 3 times, K10...32 sts.
14th row. P2tog, purl to last 2 sts, P2tog...30 sts.
Work 20 rows st st, beg with a knit row and dec one st at beg of every row...10 sts.
Work 6 rows st st.
Shape for head.
Inc one st at beg of next 8 rows...18 sts.
Cast off 3 sts at beg of next 2 rows...12 sts.
Next row. K2, inc in each of next 8 sts, K2...20 sts.
Work 5 rows st st, beg with a purl row and inc one st at each end of every row...30 sts.
Work 15 rows st st, dec one st at beg of every row...15 sts.
Next row. Purl.
Next row. *K2tog; rep from * to last st, K1...8 sts.
Next row. Purl.
Next row. (K2tog) 4 times...4 sts.
Cast off.

To sew up body
Fold in half lengthways with right sides tog. Sew row ends tog, working from tip of nose to centre of body, then from tip of tail to centre of body, leaving a large gap in centre for filling. Turn to right side and fill firmly, starting at tip of nose and working towards the middle. Fill from the tip of the tail (more filling will be added in tip of tail after the Tail Spikes have been positioned). Pin gap closed. The model's circumference should be approximately 44.5 cm at the widest part at this stage. Stitch gap closed.

ABOVE: TRICERATOPS. *BELOW:* HATCHLING AND EGG.
INSET: HATCHLING EMERGING FROM THE EGG.

STEGOSAURUS.

ABOVE: PTERODACTYL. *BELOW:* BRACHIOSAURUS.

Tyrannosaurus Rex.

FRONT LEGS

Make 2, beg at base of foot.

Using body yarn, cast on 10 sts.

1st row (right side). Inc knitways in every st...20 sts.

Work 2 rows st st, beg with a purl row.

Shape toe edge.

Purl 3 rows.★★

Work 24 rows st st, beg with a knit row.

Shape top.

Cont in st st, cast off 3 sts at beg of next 2 rows, then dec one st at each end of foll 4 rows...6 sts.

Next row. (K2tog) 3 times...3 sts. Cast off.

BACK LEFT LEG

Work as for Front Legs to ★★.

Work 18 rows st st, beg with a knit row.

Shape Knee A.

Next row. K3, (K2tog) twice, K6, inc in each of next 4 sts, K3...22 sts.

Work 11 rows st st, beg with a purl row.

Shape Knee B.

Next row. K3, inc in each of next 2 sts, K6, (K2tog) 4 times, K3...20 sts.

Next row. Purl.

Cont in st st, inc one st at each end of next and foll alt rows 6 times in all...32 sts.

Next row. Purl.

Shape top.

Cont in st st, cast off 5 sts at beg of next 2 rows, then dec one st at each end of foll 5 rows...12 sts.

Next row. Purl.

Next row. (K2tog) 6 times...6 sts.

Next row. Purl.

Next row. (K2tog) 3 times...3 sts. Cast off.

BACK RIGHT LEG

Work as for Back Left Leg, noting to work Knee A and Knee B rows as folls.

Shape Knee A.

Next row. K3, inc in each of next 4 sts, K6, (K2tog) twice, K3...22 sts.

Shape Knee B.

Next row. K3, (K2tog) 4 times, K6, inc in each of next 2 sts, K3...20 sts.

To sew up Legs

Slip a length of matching yarn through sts in cast on row, draw up tightly and fasten off for base of foot. Fold work in half lengthways, with right sides tog, and back stitch over row ends, starting at bottom of Leg and finishing at beg of top shaping. Turn to right side and fill firmly, forming a flat edge from base of foot to toe edge.

TAIL SPIKES
Make 1 small as folls.
Using 2 strands of white yarn, cast on 13 sts.
1st row. K5, inc in each of next 3 sts, K5...16 sts.
2nd row. Purl.
3rd row. K5, (K2tog) 3 times, K5...13 sts.
Cast off.

Make 1 large as folls.
Using 2 strands of white yarn, cast on 25 sts.
1st row. K11, inc in each of next 3 sts, K11...28 sts.
2nd row. Purl.
3rd row. K11, (K2tog) 3 times, K11...25 sts.
Cast off.

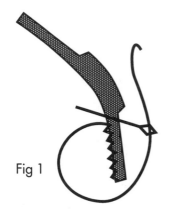

Fig 1

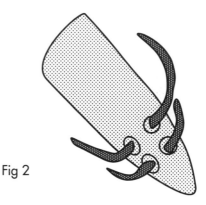

Fig 2

To sew up
Over sew cast-on and cast-off rows tog, with right side out (see fig 1). Bend into a V shape at inc sts. Insert the small Spike through first set of holes at tail tip. Insert large Spike through next set of holes in tail. Poke a little more filling around tail Spikes to strengthen and force the Spikes to stand. Stitch Spikes in place securely (see fig 2).

PLATELETS
Make 3 large as folls.
Using body yarn, cast on 20 sts.
1st row (wrong side). Purl.
2nd row. (Inc in next st, K8, inc in next st) twice...24 sts.
3rd and foll alt rows. Purl.
4th row. (Inc in next st, K10, inc in next st) twice...28 sts.
6th row. (Inc in next st, K12, inc in next st) twice...32 sts.
8th row. (Inc in next st, K14, inc in next st) twice...36 sts.
10th row. (Inc in next st, K16, inc in next st) twice...40 sts.
12th row. (Inc in next st, K18, inc

in next st) twice...44 sts.
14th row. (K2tog, K18, K2tog) twice...40 sts.
16th row. (K2tog, K16, K2tog) twice...36 sts.
18th row. (K2tog, K14, K2tog) twice...32 sts.
20th row. (K2tog, K12, K2tog) twice...28 sts.
22nd row. (K2tog, K10, K2tog) twice...24 sts.
24th row. (K2tog, K8, K2tog) twice...20 sts.
26th row. (K2tog, K6, K2tog) twice...16 sts.
28th row. (K2tog, K4, K2tog) twice...12 sts.
30th row. (K2tog) 6 times...6 sts.

Break off yarn, thread end through rem sts, draw up and fasten off securely.

Make 5 medium as folls.
Using body yarn, cast on 18 sts.
1st row (wrong side). Purl.
2nd row. (Inc in next st, K7, inc in next st) twice...22 sts.
3rd and foll alt rows. Purl.
4th row. (Inc in next st, K9, inc in next st) twice...26 sts.
6th row. (Inc in next st, K11, inc in next st) twice...30 sts.
8th row. (K2tog, K11, K2tog)

twice...26 sts.
10th row. (K2tog, K9, K2tog) twice...22 sts.
12th row. (K2tog, K7, K2tog) twice...18 sts.
14th row. (K2tog, K5, K2tog) twice...14 sts.
16th row. (K2tog, K3, K2tog) twice...10 sts.
18th row. (K2tog) 5 times...5 sts.

Break off yarn, thread end through rem sts, draw up and fasten off securely.

Make 4 small as folls.
Using body yarn, cast on 14 sts.
1st row (wrong side). Purl.
2nd row. (Inc in next st, K5, inc in next st) twice...18 sts.
3rd and foll alt rows. Purl.
4th row. (Inc in next st, K7, inc in next st) twice...22 sts.
6th row. (K2tog, K7, K2tog) twice...18 sts.
8th row. (K2tog, K5, K2tog) twice...14 sts.
10th row. (K2tog, K3, K2tog) twice...10 sts.
12th row. (K2tog) 5 times...5 sts.

Break off yarn, thread end through rem sts, draw up and fasten off securely.

To sew up
Fold in half with right sides tog and stitch rows ends, leaving cast-on edge open. Turn to right side and fill lightly, keeping pieces fairly flat.(see fig 3)

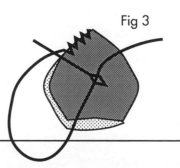

Fig 3

TO ASSEMBLE

Pin centre top edge of Front Legs 10.5 cm from centre back and in line with first neck dec row. Pin centre lower edge (leg seam) of Front Legs 3.5 cm from under-body seam and in line with first neck dec row. Pin centre top edge of Back Legs 6.5 cm from centre back and 6 cm from first body inc row. Pin centre lower edge (leg seam) of Back Legs 7 cm from under-body seam and 6 cm from first body inc row. Check for appearance and stance, adjust if necessary, then stitch in place.

For eyes, mark a position on both sides of head, 1.5 cm from centre head and 2 cm from the row where the head went from 12 sts to 20 sts. Using black yarn, work small sts over these positions for eyes.

Pin 2 rows of Platelets along centre back, starting at the base of the neck and finishing at the top of the tail. Place the large Platelets in the centre, the medium sizes either side of these, and then position one small one at the neck edge and rem 3 at the tail. Stagger the gaps between the Platelets of each row so that you cannot see between them when viewing from the side. Stitch the Platelets in place, keeping the cast-on edges slightly apart and adding a little more filling just before closing off to help the Platelets stand (see fig 4).

Fig 4

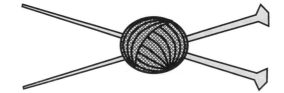

EGG AND HATCHLING

The completed Egg containing Hatchling stands approximately 14.5 cm high and 10 cm wide. The Hatchling stands approximately 9 cm high and 21 cm long.

Materials

Approximately 20 g of 8 ply yarn for Egg. Approximately 30 g of 8 ply yarn for Hatchling. Approximately 30 g of filling for Hatchling. One 10 cm long zip for Egg (to match yarn colour). A longer zip can be cut to fit (see assembly instructions). Black yarn for eyes. One pair each 3 mm and 5 mm knitting needles.

EGG

Starting at the tip.

Using 5 mm needles and 2 strands of yarn, cast on 10 sts.

1st row. ★K1, inc knitways in next st; rep from ★ to end...15 sts.

Work 3 rows st st, beg with a purl row.

5th row. ★K2, inc knitways in next st; rep from ★ to end...20 sts.

Work 3 rows st st, beg with a purl row.

9th row. ★K3, inc knitways in next st; rep from ★ to end...25 sts.

Work 3 rows st st, beg with a purl row.

13th row. ★K4, inc knitways in next st; rep from ★ to end...30 sts.

Work 3 rows st st, beg with a purl row.

25

17th row. *K5, inc knitways in next st; rep from * to end...35 sts. Work 3 rows st st, beg with a purl row.
21st row. *K6, inc knitways in next st; rep from * to end...40 sts. Work 11 rows st st, beg with a purl row.
Shape base.
1st row. (K3, K2tog) 8 times...32 sts.

2nd and foll alt rows. Purl.
3rd row. *K2, K2tog; rep from * to end...24 sts.
5th row. (K2tog) 12 times...12 sts.

Break off yarns (leaving a long length), thread ends through rem sts, draw up and fasten off securely. (see fig 1)

Fig 1

Fig 2

Fig 3

Fig 4

To sew up
Fold Egg in half lngthways, with right sides tog. Using one thread of yarn leftover from drawing up sts, stitch row ends tog, sewing upwards from the base for approximately 2 cm. Run a thread through the cast-on row and draw up to close. Stitch row ends tog from the tip of the Egg for approximately 5 cm (see fig 2). Turn right side out (see fig 3). With the zip closed, place it within the Egg with the clasp uppermost at the point you have just sewn from the top of the Egg. Pin the zip in place so the sides of the Egg almost meet (see fig 4). If the zip is too long, stitch across the tracks of the zip at the desired length and cut off rem. Open the zip, then using sewing thread stitch the sides of the zip securely in place. Test the zip for closure.

HATCHLING
TAIL, BODY AND HEAD
Worked in one piece, beg at tail.
Using 3 mm needles, cast on 5 sts.
1st row. Inc knitways in every

st..10 sts.
Work 23 rows st st, beg with a purl row.
Shape body.
1st row. K2, inc in each of next 6

sts, K2...16 sts.

Work 3 rows st st, beg with a purl row.

5th row. K3, inc in each of next 10 sts, K3...26 sts.

Work 3 rows st st, beg with a purl row.

9th row. K10, inc in each of next 6 sts, K10...32 sts.

Work 25 rows st st, beg with a purl row.

Shape for neck.

1st row. K4, (K2tog, K1) 8 times, K4...24 sts.

2nd row. Purl.

3rd row. K4, (K2tog) 8 times, K4...16 sts.

Work 3 rows st st, beg with a purl row.

Shape head.

1st row. Inc knitways in every st...32 sts.

Work 11 rows st st, beg with a purl row.

13th row. K2tog, K7, sl 1, K1,

psso, K2tog, K6, sl 1, K1, psso, K2tog, K7, K2tog...26 sts.

Work 3 rows st st, beg with a purl row.

17th row. K2tog, K5, sl 1, K1, psso, K2tog, K4, sl 1, K1, psso, K2tog, K5, K2tog...20 sts.

Work 3 rows st st, beg with a purl row.

21st row. K2tog, K3, sl 1, K1, psso, K2tog, K2, sl 1, K1, psso, K2tog, K3, K2tog...14 sts.

Work 3 rows st st, beg with a purl row.

25th row. K2tog, ★K2tog, K1; rep from ★ to end...9 sts.

Work 3 rows st st, beg with a purl row.

29th row. ★K2tog, K1; rep from ★ to end...6 sts.

Break off yarn, thread end through rem sts, draw up and fasten off securely.

To sew up body

Fold in half lengthways, with right sides tog. Sew row ends tog, working from tip of nose to centre body, then from tip of tail to centre body, leaving a large gap in centre for filling. Turn to right side and fill firmly, starting with tip of nose and tip of tail and working towards the middle. Pin gap closed. The model's circumference should be approximately 17 cm at the widest part at this stage. Stitch gap closed.

LEFT LEG

Make 2, starting at the claw.

Using 3mm needles, cast on 6 sts.

1st row. Purl.

2nd row. Inc knitways in every st...12 sts.

Work 5 rows st st, beg with a purl row.

8th row. K2, (K2tog) 3 times, K1, inc in each of next 2 sts, K1...11 sts.

Work 13 rows st st, beg with a purl row.

Shape top.

22nd row. Cast off 2 sts, knit to end...9 sts.

23rd row. Cast off 2 sts purlways, purl to end...7 sts.

Cont in st st, beg with a knit row, dec one st at beg of every row until one st rems; tie off last st.

RIGHT LEG

Make 2.

Work as for Left Leg, reversing shapings.

To sew up.

Fold Legs in half lengthways, right sides tog, and stitch row ends tog. Run a thread through cast-on edge and draw up to close. Turn to right side and fill, creating a bend at inc sts.

NECK FRILL

Using 3 mm needles, cast on 18 sts.

Work 4 rows st st, beg with a knit row.

5th row. K2tog, K5, K2tog, yfwd twice, K2tog, K5, K2tog...16 sts.

Work 3 rows st st, beg with a purl row and picking up yfwds as 2 sts.

Cast off.

To sew up

Fold Frill in half, with right sides tog, so cast-on and cast-off edges meet. Over sew row ends. Turn to right side.

TO ASSEMBLE

Position Front Legs, placing Legs 6 clear sts from centre back st and 8 rows from first neck dec row. Position Back Legs, placing Legs 4 clear sts from centre back st and 4 sts from last body inc row. Check for appearance and stance, adjust if necessary, then stitch in place.

Attach cast-on and cast-off edges of Neck Frill to head, 4 rows forward of head inc row with 'dip' at centre top.

Using black yarn, work small sts for eyes on either side of the head at the start of the dec for the nose.

Place the Hatchling head first into the top of Egg, with its underbelly towards you. Fold the Legs and tail onto the belly and under the head. Push the rear down into the base of the Egg. Close the zip and mould the Egg into a 'natural' shape (see fig 5).

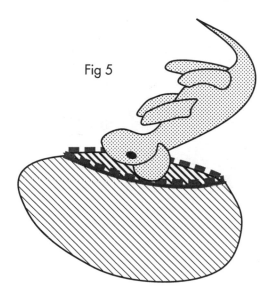

Fig 5

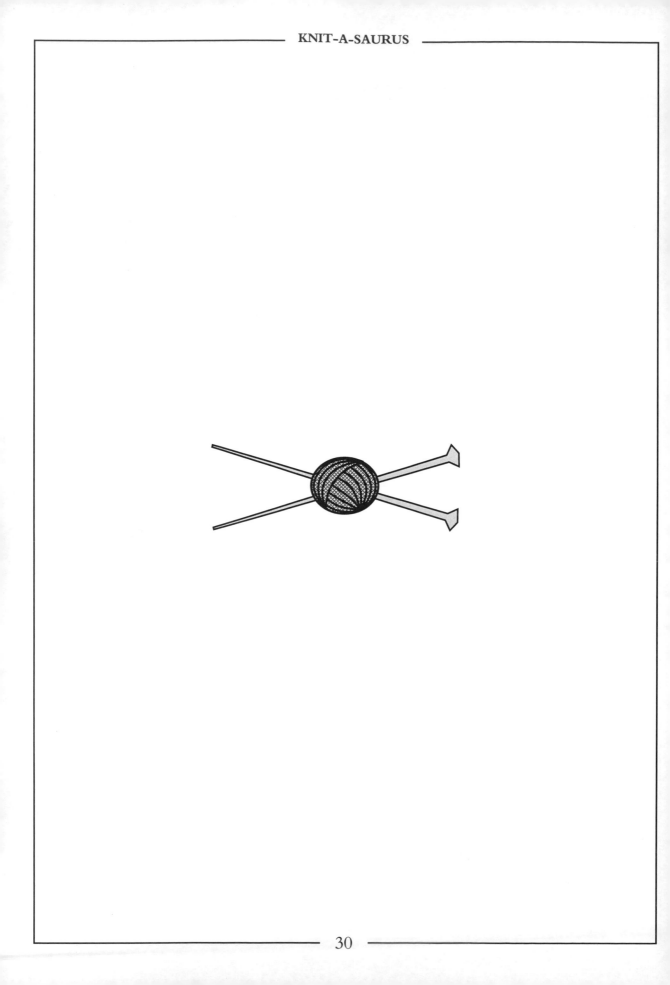

PTERODACTYL

Wing span is approximately 48 cm. Body length from beak to tail is approximately 32 cm.

Materials

Approximately 30 g yellow 8 ply yarn for body. Approximately 10 g orange 8 ply yarn for beak. Approximately 10 g brown yarn for head and crest. Approximately 40 g white yarn for wings. Remnants of black yarn for eyes. Approximately 30 g filling. One pair of 3 mm knitting needles. One coathanger for wings or, for younger children, use pipecleaners.

BODY

Starting at tail.

Using yellow yarn, cast on 4 sts.
1st row. (wrong side). Purl.
2nd row. Inc knitways in every st...8 sts.

Cont in st st, beg with a purl row, inc one st at each end of foll 4th rows until there are 36 sts.

Work 3 rows straight in st st, beg with a purl row.

62nd row. *K2, K2tog; rep from

★ to end...27 sts.
Work 3 rows st st, beg with a purl row.
66th row. ★K1, K2tog; rep from ★ to end...18 sts.
67th and foll alt rows. Purl.
68th row. Inc in each of next 2 sts, K3, (K2tog) 4 times, K3, inc in each of next 2 sts...18 sts.
70th row. Inc in first st, K4, (K2tog) 4 times, K4, inc in last st...16 sts.
72nd row. Inc in first st, K1, (K2tog) 6 times, K1, inc in last st...12 sts.
Work 9 rows st st, beg with a purl row.
Cast off.

To sew up
Fold in half lengthways, with right right sides tog. Stitch row ends tog from neck to tail, leaving a gap in centre body for filling. Turn to right side and fill firmly, particularly the neck.

HEAD

Using brown yarn, cast on 32 sts. Mark the position between the 8th and 9th sts and the 24th and 25th sts with coloured threads.
Work 14 rows st st, beg with a knit row.
15th row. ★K2, K2tog; rep from ★ to end...24 sts.
16th and foll alt rows. Purl.
17th row. ★K1, K2tog; rep from ★ to end...16 sts.
19th row. (K2tog) 8 times...8 sts.

Break off yarn, thread end through rem sts, draw up and fasten off securely.

To sew up
With right sides tog, join row ends from 8 sts fastened off to cast on edge. Turn to right side and fill in a cup shape (see fig 1).

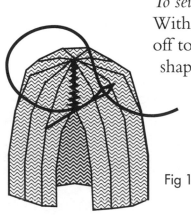

Fig 1

CREST

Beg at top.
Using brown yarn, cast on 4 sts.
1st row. Purl.
2nd row. Inc knitways in every st...8 sts.
Work 5 rows st st, beg with a purl row.
8th row. Inc in each of next 2 sts, (K2tog) twice, inc in each of last 2 sts...10 sts.
Work 5 rows st st, beg with a purl row.
14th row. K4, K2tog, K4...9 sts.
Work 25 rows st st, beg with a purl row.
Cast off.

To sew up
Run a thread through the cast-on row and draw up. With right sides tog, stitch row ends tog to form a tube with a bulbed end. Turn to right side and fill firmly, paying particular attention to a neat bulb shape at the top of the tube.

BEAK

Using orange yarn, cast on 43 sts.
Work 3 rows st st, beg with a purl row.
4th row. (K2tog, K6, sl 1, K1, psso, K1) 3 times, K2tog, K6, K2tog...35 sts.
Work 5 rows st st, beg with a purl row.
10th row. (K2tog, K4, K2tog, K1) 3 times, K2tog, K4, K2tog...27 sts.
Work 5 rows st st, beg with a purl row.
16th row. (K2tog, K2, K2tog, K1) 3 times, K2tog, K2, K2tog...19 sts.
Work 5 rows st st, beg with a purl row.
22nd row. (K2tog twice, K1) 3 times, K1, K2tog, K1...12 sts.
Work 5 rows st st, beg with a purl row.
28th row. (K2tog) 6 times...6 sts.

Break off yarn, thread end through rem sts, draw up and fasten off securely (see fig 2a below).

Fig 2a

To sew up
With right sides tog, stitch row ends tog from the drawn-up end to the cast-on edge. Turn to right side and fill firmly, encouraging a pyramid shape with four triangular sides as you fill (see fig 2b).

Fig 2b

RIGHT WING

Starting at top of Wing.
Using 2 strands of white yarn, cast on 71 sts.
1st row. K18, inc in each of next 3 sts, K21, inc in each of next 5 sts, K24...79 sts.
Work 3 rows st st, beg with a purl row.
5th row. K18, (K2tog) 3 times, K21, (K2tog) 5 times, K24...71 sts.

Break off one strand of yarn.

★★Next row. Purl.
Next row. Inc in first st, knit to last 2 sts, K2tog.
Next row. Purl.★★
9th row. Inc in first st, K19, K2tog, K21, K2tog, K24, K2tog...69 sts.
Work as from ★★ to ★★.
13th row. Inc in first st, K20, K2tog, K20, K2tog, K22, K2tog...67 sts.
Work as from ★★ to ★★.
17th row. Inc in first st, K21, K2tog, K19, K2tog, K20, K2tog...65 sts.
Work as from ★★ to ★★.
21st row. Inc in first st, K22, K2tog, K18, K2tog, K18, K2tog...63 sts.
Work as from ★★ to ★★.
25th row. Inc in first st, K23, K2tog, K17, K2tog, K16, K2tog...61 sts.
Work as from ★★ to ★★.
29th row. Inc in first st, K24, K2tog, K16, K2tog, K14, K2tog...59 sts.
Work as from ★★ to ★★.
33rd row. Inc in first st, K25, K2tog, K15, K2tog, K12, K2tog...57 sts.
Work as from ★★ to ★★.
37th row. Inc in first st, K26, K2tog, K14, K2tog, K10, K2tog...55 sts.
Cast off.

LEFT WING

Work as for Right Wing, reversing shapings.

To sew up

With wrong sides tog, fold cast-on edge over to where Wing changes to one thread; stitch in place. Encourage a natural bend in the edge at the junctions where st incs were worked. If the back edge of the Wing curls too much, very lightly touch with a warm iron (see fig 3).

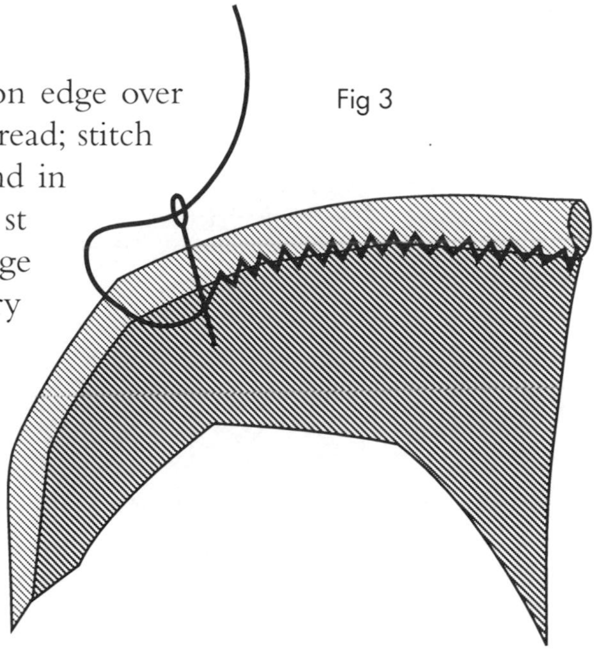

Fig 3

TO ASSEMBLE

You will notice four lines running through the Beak from the tip of the Beak to the cast-on edge. Place cast-on edge of Beak over first 2 rows on caston edge of Head, matching the Beak seam with the Head seam. Match the lines either side of this to the coloured thread markers. Using brown yarn, stitch in place, adding a little more filling before closing.

Fig 4

Using brown yarn, attach the Crest to top of Head, placing it in the centre at the first dec row of the Head shaping (see fig 4).

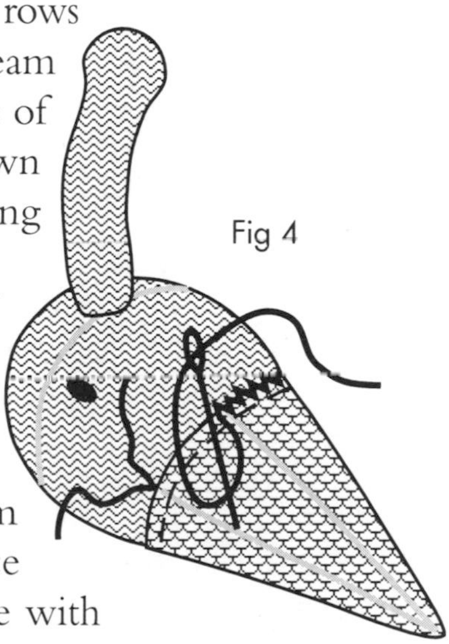

To attach the Head to the Body, mark a position on the base of the Head 1.5 cm from the Head Beak seam along the Head seam. Place the open neck edge over this and stitch in place with brown yarn, adding more filling before closing to add strength (see fig 5).

Cut coathanger wire to give a 34 cm length, push through body at 2nd row of dec on lower neck, matching centre of wire with centre of neck. Alternatively, join pipecleaners to create a 34 cm length. Thread cast-on hem of Wings over wire, bending wire at incs to form 'wing' shapes. Stitch inside edge of Wings to Body along a column of sts, leaving 6 clear sts from

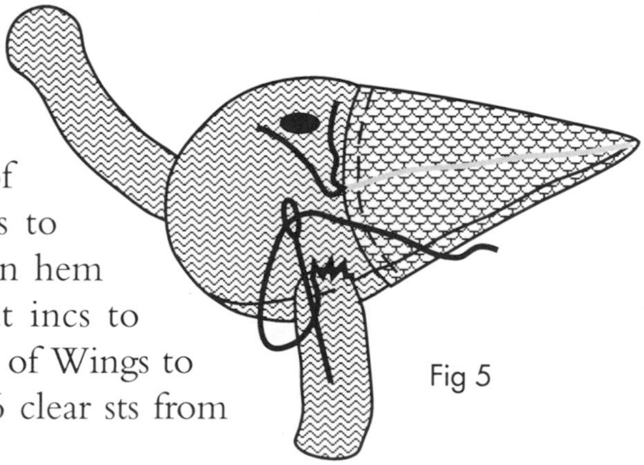

Fig 5

centre back st and matching top of Wing with the 2nd row of neck dec (see fig 6).

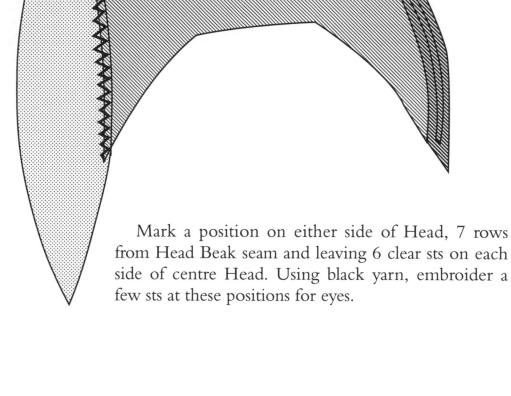

Fig 6

Mark a position on either side of Head, 7 rows from Head Beak seam and leaving 6 clear sts on each side of centre Head. Using black yarn, embroider a few sts at these positions for eyes.

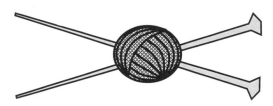

TYRANNOSAURUS REX

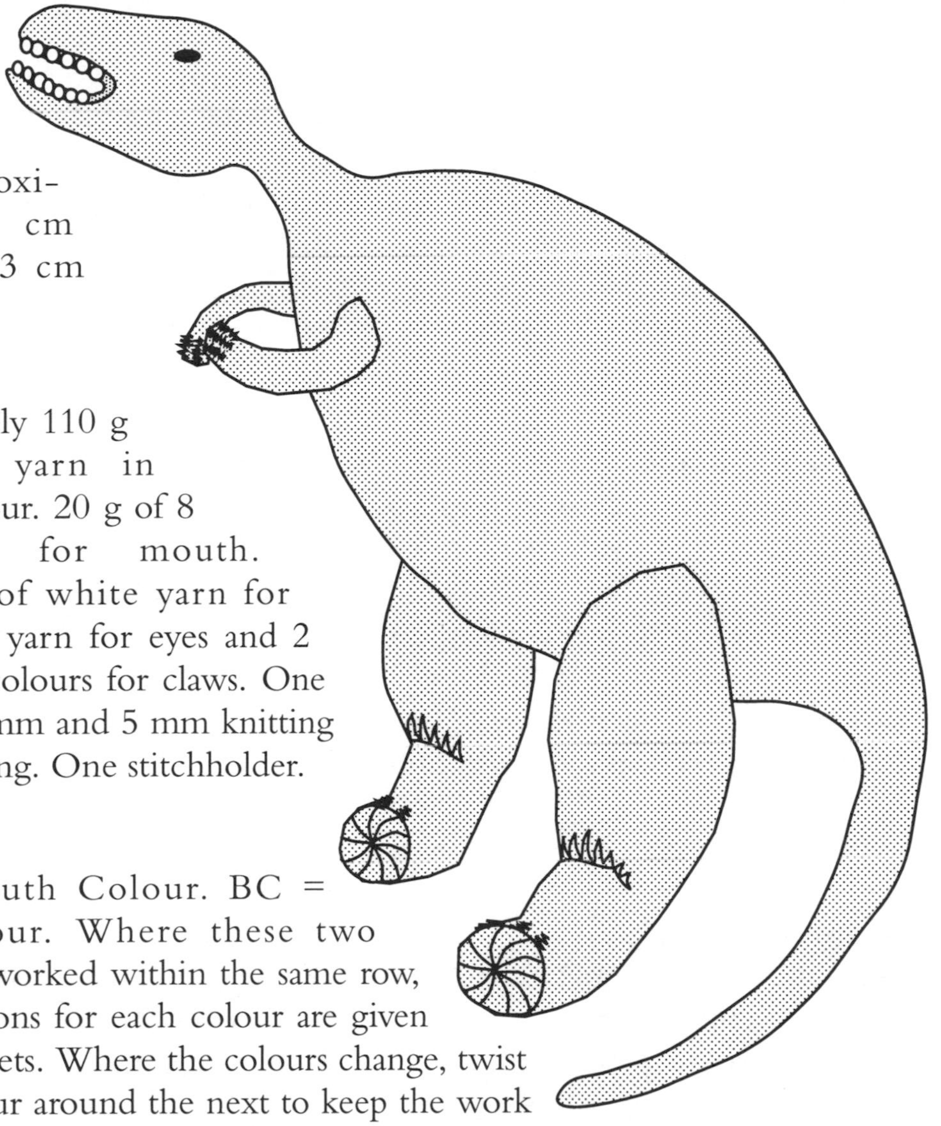

This model stands approximately 43 cm high and 63 cm long.

Materials
Approximately 110 g of 8 ply yarn in selected colour. 20 g of 8 ply yarn for mouth. Remnants of white yarn for teeth, black yarn for eyes and 2 contrasting colours for claws. One pair each 3 mm and 5 mm knitting needles. Filling. One stitchholder.

Special note
MC = Mouth Colour. BC = Body Colour. Where these two colours are worked within the same row, the instructions for each colour are given within brackets. Where the colours change, twist the last colour around the next to keep the work tight and prevent holes (see fig 1). Use separate balls of colour for each section. Familiarise yourself with what is happening in the shaping of the head before starting the pieces. The mouth floor is added in the middle of the Lower Jaw and the roof of the mouth at the beginning of the Upper Jaw.

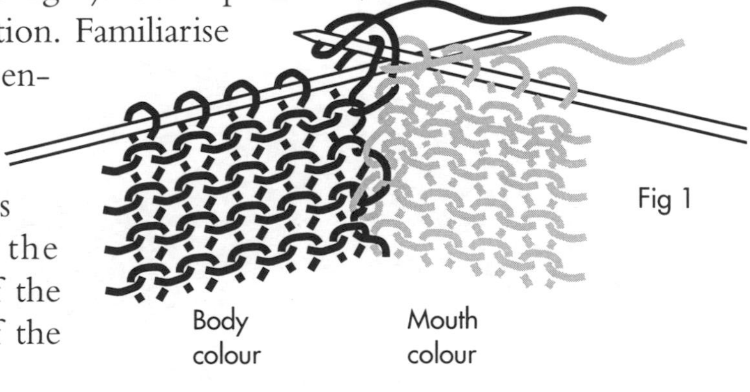

Fig 1

Body colour

Mouth colour

TAIL, BODY, NECK AND HEAD

Worked in one piece (to jaws), beg at tip of tail.

Using BC and 3 mm needles, cast on 6 sts.

Work in st st, beg with a knit row, inc one st at each end of 1st and every foll 12th row until there are 16 sts, then at each end of every foll 4th row row until there are 30 sts.

Next row. Purl.

Shape for body.

Next row. Inc in each of next 10 sts, K10, inc in each of next 10 sts...50 sts.

Work 3 rows st st, beg with a purl row.

5th row. Inc in each of next 5 sts, K40, inc in each of next 5 sts...60 sts.

Work 49 rows st st, beg with a purl row.

Shape shoulders.

1st row. *K6, (K2tog) twice; rep from * to end...48 sts.

Work 9 rows st st, beg with a purl row.

11th row. *K7, inc in next st; rep from * to end...54 sts.

Work 13 rows st st, beg with a purl row.

Shape for neck.

1st row. *K4, K2tog; rep from * to end...45 sts.

2nd and foll alt rows. Purl.

3rd row. *K3, K2tog; rep from * to end...36 sts.

5th row. *K2, K2tog; rep from * to end...27 sts.

7th row. Inc in each of next 3 sts, K2, (K2tog) 4 times, K1, (K2tog) 4 times, K2, inc in each of next 3 sts...25 sts.

Work 21 rows st st, beg with a purl row.

29th row. (K2tog) twice, inc in each of next 17 sts, (K2tog) twice...38 sts.

Work 15 rows st st, beg with a purl row and inc one st at beg of each row...53 sts.

45th row. Inc in next st, K19, (K2tog) 3 times, K1, (K2tog) 3 times, K19, inc in next st...49 sts.

46th row. Purl.

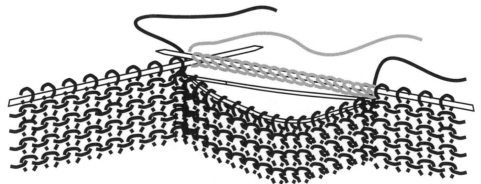

Fig 2 – Dividing for lower jaw

Divide for Lower Jaw (see fig 2).

1st row. K12, slip next 25 sts on a stitch holder and leave at front of work, join in MC and cast on 15 sts in MC, join in second ball of BC and knit last 12 sts in BC...39 sts.

Cont on these 39 sts, work 3 rows st st, beg with a purl row and keeping colours correct as set.

5th row. (K2tog, K10) in BC, (K5, K2tog, K1, K2tog, K5) in MC, (K10, K2tog) in BC...35 sts.

Work 3 rows st st, beg with a purl row and keeping colours correct as set in last row.

9th row. (K2tog, K9) in BC, (K4, K2tog, K1, K2tog, K4) in MC, (K9, K2tog) in BC...31 sts.

Work 3 rows st st, beg with a purl row and keeping colours correct as set in last row.

13th row. (K2tog, K8) in BC, (K3, K2tog, K1, K2tog, K3) in MC, (K8, K2tog) in BC...27 sts.

Work 3 rows st st, beg with a purl row and keeping colours correct as set in last row.

17th row. (K2tog, K7) in BC, (K2, K2tog, K1, K2tog, K2) in MC, (K7, K2tog) in BC...23 sts.

Work 3 rows st st, beg with a purl row and keeping colours correct as set in last row.

21st row. (K2tog, K6) in BC, (K1, K2tog, K1, K2tog, K1) in MC, (K6, K2tog) in BC...19 sts.

Work 3 rows st st, beg with a purl row and keeping colours correct as set in last row.

25th row. (K2tog, K5) in BC, (K2tog, K1, K2tog) in MC, (K5, K2tog) in BC...15 sts.

26th row. Purl in colours as set.

27th row. Cast off 6 sts in BC, break off MC and knit next 2 sts in BC (there should be 3 sts on needle), then use second strand of BC to knit rem 6 sts...9 sts.

28th row. Cast off 6 sts purlways, break off second strand of BC, use first strand to purl to end...3 sts.

Using first strand of BC only, work 5 rows st st to form flap.

Cast off.

Work Upper Jaw.

Using MC and 3 mm needles, cast on 15 sts, then join in BC and knit across right side of 25 sts from stitch holder...40 sts.

Work 7 rows st st, beg with a purl row and keeping colours correct as set.

9th row. (K5, K2tog, K1, K2tog, K5) in MC, (K5, K2tog, knit to last 7 sts, K2tog, K5) in BC...36 sts.

Work 3 rows st st, beg with a purl row and keeping colours correct as set in last row.

13th row. (K4, K2tog, K1, K2tog, K4) in MC, (K5, K2tog, knit to last 7 sts, K2tog, K5) in BC...32 sts.

Work 3 rows st st, beg with a purl row and keeping colours correct as set in last row.

17th row. (K3, K2tog, K1, K2tog, K3) in MC, (K5, K2tog, knit to last 7 sts, K2tog, K5) in BC...28 sts.

Work 3 rows st st, beg with a purl row and keeping colours correct as set in last row.

21st row. (K2, K2tog, K1, K2tog, K2) in MC, (K5, K2tog, knit to last 7 sts, K2tog, K5) in BC...24 sts.

Work 3 rows st st, beg with a purl row and keeping colours correct as set in last row.

25th row. (K1, K2tog, K1, K2tog, K1) in MC, (K5, K2tog, knit to last 7 sts, K2tog, K5) in BC...20 sts.

Work 3 rows st st, beg with a purl row and keeping colours correct as set in last row.

29th row. (K2tog, K1, K2tog) in MC, (K5, K2tog, K1, K2tog, K5) in BC...16 sts.

30th row. Using BC only from now to end, cast off 5 sts purlways, purl to end...11 sts.

31st row. Cast off 8 sts, knit rem 2 sts in BC...3 sts.

Beg with a purl row, work 3 rows st st to form flap.

Cast off.

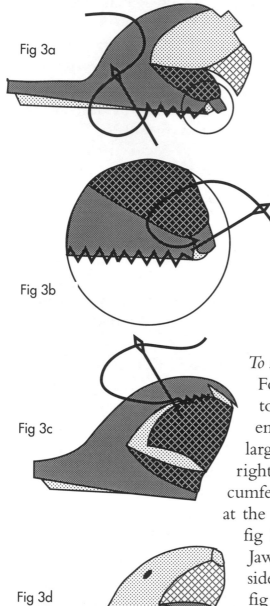

Fig 3a

Fig 3b

Fig 3c

Fig 3d

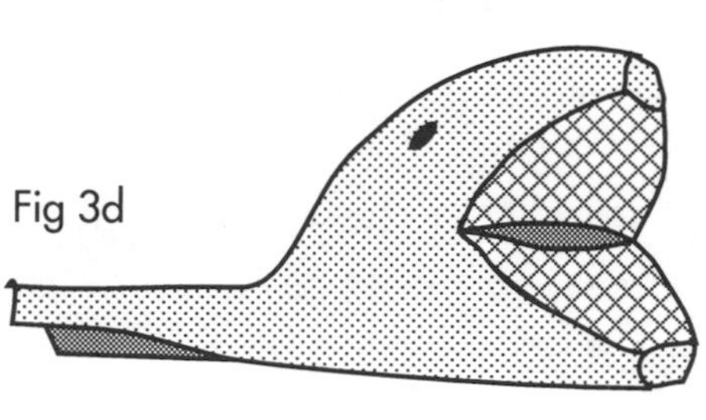

To sew up body

Fold in half lengthways with right sides tog. Beg at the tip of the tail, stitch row ends tog up to the lower neck, leaving a large gap for turning and filling. Turn to right side and fill firmly. The model's circumference should be approximately 40 cm at the widest part. With wrong side out (see fig 3a), stitch the row ends of the Lower Jaw tog, then fold up the flap and stitch sides to the 6 sts cast off on each side (see fig 3b). Turn right side out (see fig 3c). With right sides tog, stitch row ends of Upper Jaw piece tog, then stitch sides of flap to the sts at the cast-off side. Turn right side out (see fig 3d). From inside at the rear of the mouth, join the Lower Jaw to the Upper Jaw. Fill head and jaws firmly (keeping the shape of the head), then oversew rem of neck to enclose filling.

TEETH

Make 2 sets (see fig 4).
Using 5 mm needles and 2 strands of white yarn, cast on 26 sts.
1st row. Knit.
2nd row. K2tog, *yfwd, K2tog; rep from * to end...25 sts.
3rd row. Knit.

Break off 1 strand of yarn, then cast off with the other.

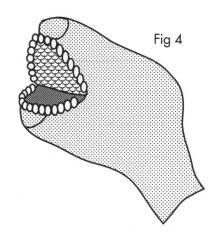

Fig 4

To sew up
Fold in half, with right sides out, over sew cast-on and cast-off edges tog. Fold in half to find centre and mark centre with a pin. Pin over-sewn edge of one set of Teeth to centre of Upper Jaw, and the other set to centre of Lower Jaw, placing them along edge where BC and MC meet. Stitch in place.

LEFT BACK LEG

Beg at base of foot.
Using BC and 3 mm needles, cast on 8 sts.
1st row. Inc knitways in every st...16 sts.
Work 2 rows st st, beg with a purl row.
Shape toe edge.
Purl 3 rows.
Work 8 rows st st, beg with a knit row.

15th row. K2, inc in each of next 4 sts, K4, (K2tog) twice, K2...18 sts.
Work 7 rows st st, beg with a purl row.
23rd row. K2, (K2tog) 4 times, K4, inc in each of next 2 sts, K2...16 sts.
Work 13 rows st st, beg with a purl row.
37th row. K2, (K2tog) twice, K4, inc in each of next 4 sts, K2...18 sts.

38th row. Purl.

39th row. K2, K2tog, K6, inc in each of next 4 sts, K4...21 sts.

Work 3 rows st st, beg with a purl row.

43rd row. K2, inc in each of next 4 sts, K15...25 sts.

Work 13 rows st st, beg with a purl row and inc one st at beg of each row...38 sts.

Shape top.

Cast off 5 sts at beg of next 2 rows...28 sts.

Work 16 rows st st, beg with a knit row and dec one st at beg of each row...12 sts.

75th row. ★K1, K2tog; rep from ★ to end...8 sts.

76th row. Purl.

77th row. (K2tog) 4 times...4 sts. Cast off.

RIGHT BACK LEG

Work as for Left Back Leg, reversing shapings.

To sew up Legs

Slip a length of matching yarn through sts in cast-on row, draw up tightly and fasten off to form base of foot. Fold work in half lengthways, with right sides tog, and back-stitch over row ends, starting at bottom of Leg and finishing at beg of top shaping. Turn to right side and fill firmly, forming a flat edge from base of foot to toe edge. For claws (see fig 5), embroider 3 tapered triangular shapes in a contrasting colour on centre front of each foot. Over sew a few sts of another contrasting colour on top to define claws.

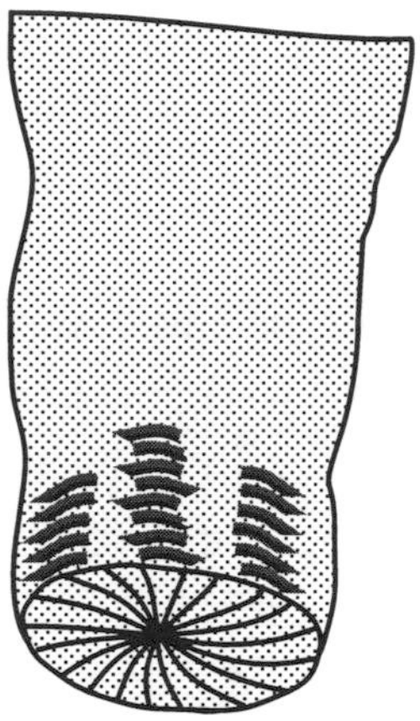

Fig 5

FRONT LIMBS

Make 2.

Using BC and 3mm needles, cast on 14 sts.

1st row. K5, inc in each of next 4 sts, K5...18 sts.

Work 9 rows st st, beg with a purl row.

11th row. K5, (K2tog) 4 times, K5...14 sts.

Cast off.

To sew up

With right sides out, fold cast-off and cast-on edges to meet and stitch tog (see fig 6). Fill from each end and bend at inc sts to create a V shape. Run a thread around row ends and draw up to close; secure thread into work. A few loops of a contrasting colour can be added to one end to create claws.

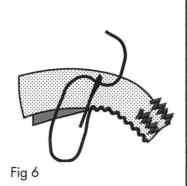

Fig 6

TO ASSEMBLE

Position Front Limbs 2 cm either side of the central chest point and in line with the first neck dec row. Position Back Legs, placing centre top edge of Legs 10 cm from centre back and 12.5 cm from body inc row, and lower edge (leg seam) 2.5 cm from under-body seam and 5 cm from body inc row. Pin in position, check for appearance and stance, adjust if necessary, then stitch in place. This model uses the bend in the tail to give it a third point for balance, so ensure the Legs are filled quite firmly.

Using black yarn, work small sts for eyes on either side of head where Upper Jaw shaping commences.

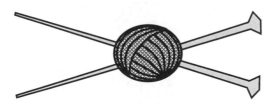